W9-BMM-009

Math Art

Projects and Activities

by Carolyn Ford Brunetto

SCHOLASTIC
PROFESSIONAL BOOKS

NEW YORK • TORONTO • LONDON • AUCKLAND • SYDNEY

To my mother and father, who always encouraged me
to be both creative and practical.

Scholastic Inc. grants teachers permission to photocopy the activity sheets from this book for classroom use. No other part of this publication may be reproduced in whole or in part, or stored in a retrieval system, or transmitted in any form or by any means, electronic, mechanical, photocopying, recording, or otherwise, without written permission of the publisher. For information regarding permission, write to Scholastic Inc., 555 Broadway, New York, NY 10012.

Cover design by Vincent Ceci and Jaime Lucero
Cover art by Carolyn Ford Brunetto
Interior design by Béatrice Schafroth
Interior photographs by Donnelly Marks
Interior illustrations by Teresa Anderko

ISBN # 0-590-96371-6
Copyright © 1997 by Carolyn Ford Brunetto
All rights reserved.
Printed in the U.S.A.

36 35 34 33 32 31 30   15 16/0

Contents

GEOMETRY

NUMBERS & COMPUTATION

MEASUREMENT

PATTERNS

STATISTICS

FRACTIONS

Introduction

Why math and art? I think the combination is a natural. After all, math is every-where, even in art—and children are naturally creative. What better way for your students to learn or practice math concepts than through exciting art experiences in which they create colorful and decorative projects that they can keep for them-selves, give as gifts, or share at home!

There's more to the math and art connection, however, than just tapping into your students' innate creativity. Many children are simply better at understanding and retaining abstract mathematical concepts through physical experiences rather than through the typical pencil-and-paper drills. In fact, the National Council of Teachers of Mathematics, in their K-4 Curriculum Standards, recommends active, hands-on learning, using concrete materials as one of the major directives in math education for the 21st century.

The 31 activities in this book will give your students lots of opportunities to express themselves visually while using meaningful math skills such as computation, geometry, measurement, fractions, and statistics. Who knows—they may even find that they're having so much fun "doing art" that they forget they're in math class at all!

As a fan of both art and of math (I've worked as a graphic designer and as a children's math magazine editor), I truly enjoyed combining my interests in math and art to create the activities in this book. I hope that, through these projects, you and your students will discover and enjoy the art in math and the math in art!

— *Carolyn Ford Brunetto*

Tips for Successful Classroom Math/Art Projects

Before students start a project . . .

◆ Try to make a sample of each project before they do. Making your own project will better help you guide students through the process, and it will alert you to any parts of the process that may be a challenge for them. If you're using your sample project as a model, try not to make it look too perfect—students may not feel that they can achieve the same results.

◆ Assemble the materials for each project before class begins, and decide how you will distribute them. Small groups may be able to use a common area, while larger groups may require that you put the correct materials on each student's desk before class time.

While your students are working . . .

◆ Set a time limit for each project, leaving enough time at the end of class for clean-up. Students who are not finished can work on their projects during free time or after school.

◆ Watch and listen to students as they work. Some of them might be able to share valuable tips, shortcuts, or mistakes with the rest of the class.

◆ If students are taking materials from a common area, check it periodically for spills or depleted supplies.

◆ Creative exploration is the goal of any art project! Encourage students to try a project a different way (as long as you feel that they are getting the same math benefits).

After your students have finished a project . . .

◆ Make sure everyone knows what he or she is responsible for during cleanup, or assign specific students to certain tasks on a rotating basis.

◆ Jot down some of your thoughts about how students handled the project. Write your notes on the same page as the project directions—that way you'll be able to adjust the project as necessary when you do the project again the following school year.

◆ Have students write about their experience with the project in their math journals—their entries are a great assessment tool for you!

◆ Over the school year, periodically display students' work in a public area of your school.

Projects by NCTM Standards

This index organizes the projects in this book according to the math standards established by the National Council of Teachers of Mathematics (NCTM). After you have introduced different math concepts to students, use these projects as follow-ups to reinforce and practice them.

Standard 10: Measurement

Standard 11: Statistics and Probability

Standard 12: Fractions and Decimals

Standard 13: Patterns and Relationships

Projects by Season and Holiday

This index will help you make meaningful seasonal and holiday connections with your math curriculum.

Geometry

PYRAMID GIFT BOXES

These pretty boxes are perfect for holding small gifts!

WHAT YOU NEED

◆ Pyramid Gift Box Pattern for each student (reproducible page 12)

◆ construction paper or any other type of heavy decorative paper

◆ scissors

◆ glue or tape

WHAT TO DO

Student Instructions / *Teacher Notes*

1. **Cut out your gift box pattern along the solid lines. Do not cut on the dotted lines.**

2. **Attach the pattern to the back of your colored paper using two or three rolled pieces of tape. (The sticky side should face out.)**

If students are using construction paper, it won't matter which side they tape the pattern to. If they are using decorative paper, they should tape the pattern to the blank side.

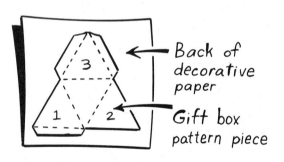

Back of decorative paper

Gift box pattern piece

3. **Cut around the solid edges of the pattern.**

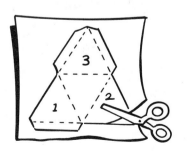

4. **Lay the colored paper cutout pattern-side-up. Carefully fold the paper and pattern along the dotted lines.**

All of the folding should be done so that the pattern is on the inside of the pyramid, and the decorative paper is on the outside. The folds will be crisper if students rub them flat with a pencil.

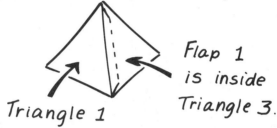

Fold sides toward pattern piece.

5. **Carefully remove the pattern from the colored paper. Glue the flap of Triangle 1 to the inside of Triangle 2.**

Make sure that the outside edges of Triangle 1 and Triangle 2 match up.

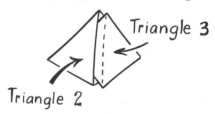

Triangle 1

Flap 1 is inside Triangle 3.

6. **Your pyramid box is ready to use. To close the box, tuck the flaps of Triangle 3 into the edges of Triangle 1 and Triangle 2.**

Triangle 3

Triangle 2

TIPS FOR A SUCCESSFUL PROJECT

◆ Make sure the inside flap of Triangle 1 is securely fastened to Triangle 2—otherwise, the box will not keep its shape.

WANT TO KEEP GOING?

◆ Use a photocopier to make larger and smaller versions of the gift box pattern. Your students will then be able to create a series of three nesting pyramid boxes!

PYRAMID GIFT BOX PATTERN

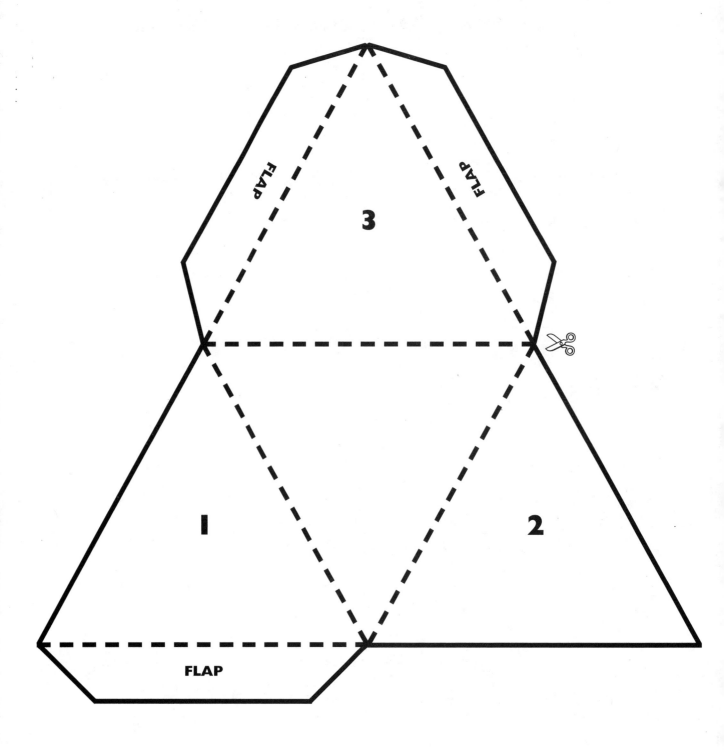

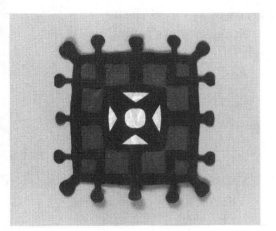

STAINED GLASS WINDOWS

These translucent designs will shed some light on geometric shapes!

WHAT YOU NEED

◆ a sheet of dark-colored construction paper for each student—the larger, the better

◆ tissue paper in various colors (scraps are fine)

◆ glue or tape

◆ scissors

WHAT TO DO

Student Instructions / *Teacher Notes*

1. Fold your sheet of construction paper in half, then in half again, then diagonally.

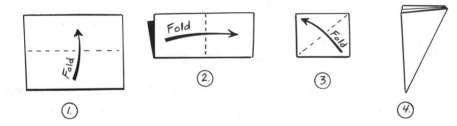

2. Start cutting out small shapes from all three sides of your triangle and from the bottom point.

Here are some ideas that will help students experiment with different shapes in their window designs. (Remind them to make sure they leave some folded edges of the triangle intact, or else the window will fall apart when they unfold it.)

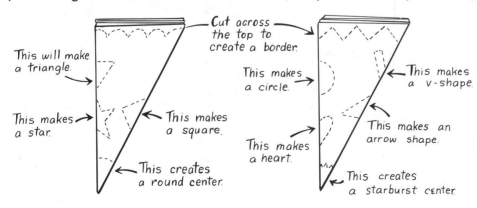

3. Carefully unfold your window. Glue or tape pieces of colored tissue paper over the open shapes. Then attach your "stained glass" window to a real window and let the sun stream though the shapes!

Back of "window".

Tape tissue paper over each open shape.

TIPS FOR A SUCCESSFUL PROJECT

◆ Students may want to practice cutting shapes out of folded plain paper before they begin the project. That way, they can decide exactly which shapes they would like to use in their window designs, and where they want to position them.

WANT TO KEEP GOING?

◆ To create even more shapes in the window designs, have your students add one more diagonal fold to the sheet of paper. (You may have to switch to larger, thinner sheets of paper to do this.)

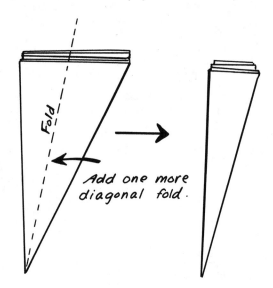

Fold

Add one more diagonal fold.

NATURE SYMMETRY PRINTS

This project will help students see the symmetry that is found in so much of nature.

WHAT YOU NEED

◆ construction paper

◆ tissue paper or tracing paper

◆ crayons, colored pencils, or grease pencils (dark colors work best)

◆ large tree leaves

WHAT TO DO

Student Instructions / *Teacher Notes*

1. **Look for a big, flat leaf on the ground. Make sure that the leaf is whole and has no nicks or holes.**

Steer students away from leaves that are not flat or have curled points at the end. Also, try to find leaves that have prominent veins. You may want to gather a group of suitable leaves yourself and bring them into class.

2. **Lay the leaf on a flat surface so that its veins are facing up. Tape the top and bottom of the leaf to the flat surface. Then tape a sheet of tissue paper over the entire leaf.**

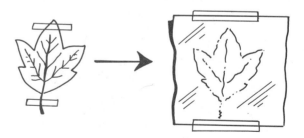

3. **Rub the crayon firmly across the tissue paper over the leaf. (Don't press too hard, or you'll tear the tissue paper or squish the leaf!) Rub the crayon back and forth in the same direction.**

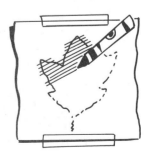

4. **When you have rubbed over the whole leaf, remove the tissue paper. Then create a frame for your picture with construction paper.**

The frames need not be square—encourage your students to try out circles and triangles, too. To make frames, have students fold sheets of construction-paper rectangles, squares, or circles in half, cut out a smaller shape from the center, and unfold.

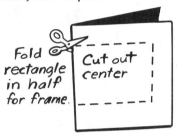

5. **Hang your symmetry print on a window!**

Ask students to find the symmetrical patterns of the leaves. Point out that the veins and edges of one half of the leaf are almost a mirror image of the opposite half.

TIPS FOR A SUCCESSFUL PROJECT

◆ The softer and darker the crayons, the easier it will be to bring up the details of the leaves.

WANT TO KEEP GOING?

◆ Nature's symmetry doesn't stop at leaves—students can also make prints of shells, flowers, plants, and even insects and butterflies.

◆ Have your students look up leaves in an encyclopedia to see more examples of leaf symmetry.

SYMMETRY POP-UP CARDS

These 3-D greeting cards are a fun way for students to explore symmetry— and they're sure to impress the lucky recipients.

WHAT YOU NEED

◆ construction paper

◆ crayons or markers

◆ scissors

WHAT TO DO

Student Instructions / *Teacher Notes*

1. **Choose two square or rectangular sheets of construction paper, and fold them in half. Set one aside to be your card. The second sheet will form your pop-up.**

2. **Draw a pop-up design along the fold of the second sheet. You will only need to draw one half of the design. Include a notched flap along the bottom of the design.**

Here are some ideas for pop-up designs:

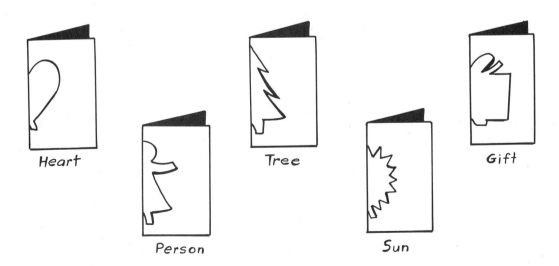

Heart Person Tree Sun Gift

3. Cut out your pop-up design. You'll notice that it has *symmetry*— it looks exactly the same on both sides.

4. Place the pop-up along the inside fold of your card. The inside fold of the pop-up should face you. Fold the flaps away from you.

5. Tape the flaps to the card at an angle. When you close the card, the pop-up should fold flat. When you open the card, the pop-up should pop up!

The pop-ups work best when both sides are taped at about a 45-degree angle.

6. Decorate your card and give it to someone you love!

TIPS FOR A SUCCESSFUL PROJECT

◆ Students may need your assistance in taping their pop-ups to their cards at the correct angle.

WANT TO KEEP GOING?

◆ Add more pop-ups to each card. Just be sure to place taller pop-ups behind smaller ones.

◆ Students can add some intricacy to their pop-ups by cutting out other shapes from their centers.

Cut out another shape from center.

AMAZING PAPER ORNAMENTS

These stretchy shapes will introduce your students to a type of geometry called topology—the study of surfaces.

WHAT YOU NEED

◆ construction paper or any decorative paper (try metallic paper for holiday time)

◆ string or yarn

◆ scissors

WHAT TO DO

Student Instructions / *Teacher Notes*

1. Cut out a round or square piece of construction paper. Your shape should measure about five inches across.

2. Fold the shape in half diagonally, then in half again.

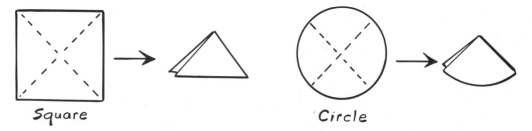

Square   Circle

3. Start cutting lines from right to left, then from left to right. Don't cut completely through any folds! Cut straight lines in a square, and curved lines in a circle.

The more cuts your students make in their shapes, the longer they'll stretch.

Square

Circle

4. Unfold your ornament and gently stretch it out. Isn't it amazing? Hang your ornament by threading string or yarn through a small hole, and knotting it at the end.

TIPS FOR A SUCCESSFUL PROJECT

◆ Avoid using thin or fragile paper for this activity—it tends to rip when the ornament is stretched.

◆ For an unusual effect, use paper that's a different color on each side.

WANT TO KEEP GOING?

◆ The stretchiness of the ornaments will vary according to the size of the original shape and the proximity of the cuts. Encourage students to experiment with these variables.

◆ Here's another fun topology paper trick: Hand out a tiny piece of paper (as small as three inches wide) to each student and say, "I'll bet that you can walk right through this tiny piece of paper." You'll win the bet—here's how:

Fold the paper in half and make as many cuts as possible, alternating from top to bottom and bottom to top. Then unfold the paper and make one more cut across the middle.

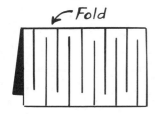

Unfold paper.
Make one more
cut across middle rows.

Your students will be amazed to find that the paper can now be stretched into a ring that is big enough to walk right through!

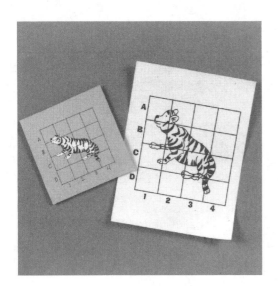

COPYCAT COORDINATES

Coordinate geometry helps students reproduce and enlarge their favorite artwork!

WHAT YOU NEED

◆ a ruler marked in inches

◆ Copycat Grid Pattern for each student (reproducible page 24)

◆ artwork drawn in a simple style, such as coloring-book art, comic-strip art, art on worksheets, greeting-card art, or sports-team logos. (Don't use photographs or complicated images.)

WHAT TO DO

Student Instructions / *Teacher Notes*

1. **Choose the image you would like to copy. The simpler the image, the easier it will be to copy. You will need to draw over the image, so don't choose a picture that you want to save.**

2. **Draw a grid over the image. Your grid should be four inches across and four inches down. It will have 16 squares. Some squares on the grid may be blank.**

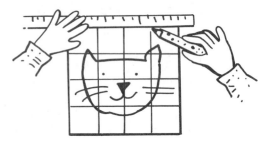

3. **Label your grid from A to D along the left side and from 1 to 4 along the bottom.**

   Be sure that students label their grids in the same way as the labels on the reproducible.

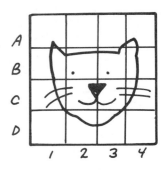

4. **Now use the coordinates to draw each square of the image's grid on your blank grid.**

Explain to students that each square on the grid is the intersection of a letter and a number, and that the letter and number combinations are called coordinates. For example, the coordinates "A-4" refer to the square that is the intersection of the "A" row and the "4" column.

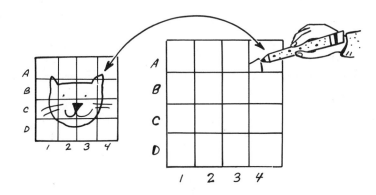

TIPS FOR A SUCCESSFUL PROJECT

◆ Some students may have trouble measuring and drawing their grids. They can start by tracing the corner of a book over their artwork—this will give them a squared-off starting point for measuring.

◆ Another solution, if you have the materials, is to copy a 4-by-4-inch grid (with coordinates) on clear acetate and let your students tape it over their artwork.

WANT TO KEEP GOING?

◆ Students can transfer their images to any size grid, as long it is a 4-by-4 square. Try working as a class to transfer a funny cartoon character or your school mascot onto a 4-by-4-foot mural!

COPYCAT GRID PATTERN

	1	2	3	4
A				
B				
C				
D				

GRAPH A WALL HANGING

Two-dimensional graphing is the key to making this three-dimensional wall hanging!

WHAT YOU NEED

◆ Wall Hanging Pattern (reproducible page 28) or a sheet of graph paper with ½-inch squares for each student

◆ wooden or plastic beads in a variety of colors—the beads must all be the same size (See Resources, page 95, for sources.)

◆ colored pencils, markers, or crayons that match the colors of the beads

◆ two sticks or dowels for each student— the length will depend on the size of the beads

◆ yarn or string

WHAT TO DO
Student Instructions / *Teacher Notes*

1. **Use the colored pencils to draw a design on your graph. Each square you color will become one colored bead on your wall hanging.**

If your students are using graph paper, have them mark off a section that is ten squares deep and eight squares wide. Then have them draw a line separating each vertical column of ten squares. Your students' designs can be abstract or representational.

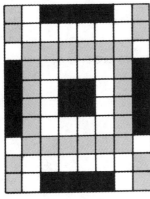

Abstract

Representational

2. Cut eight lengths of string. Tie one end of each string tightly around one of your sticks. Be sure you have enough room between the strings for the beads to fit in a row.

The length of the stick should be a few inches longer on both ends than a row of eight beads. If you're using one-inch beads, the sticks should be about a foot long. If you're using smaller beads, use shorter sticks. The length of the string should be a few inches longer than a row of the beads laid end to end.

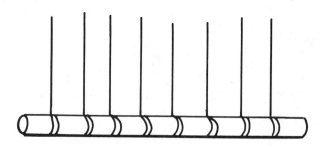

3. Use your graph as a pattern for the beads on your wall hanging. Follow the colors on each row of your pattern to figure out which beads you will need. String one row at a time. When you finish a row of ten beads, tie a knot at the end of the string.

Be sure that students are following the pattern from bottom to top as they string each row of beads. They should check each row before moving on to the next. If they're having trouble getting the string through the bead holes, wrap a piece of tape around the end of the string, or wrap a twist tie around the end of the string and use it as a needle.

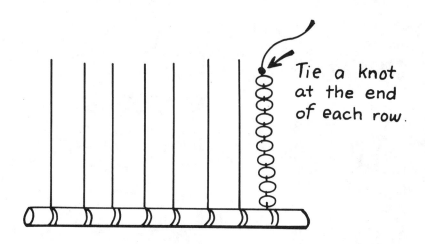

Tie a knot at the end of each row.

4. Follow your graph pattern until you have strung all eight rows of beads. Then tie the top of each string to the other stick. Cut off any extra string.

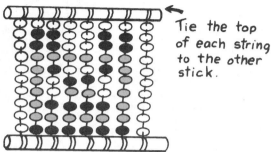

Tie the top of each string to the other stick.

5. Tie another string to your top stick to use as a hanger. Decorate the bottom stick with string tassels if you like.

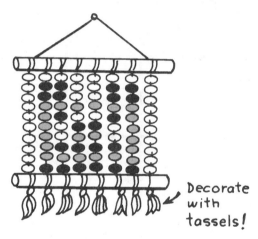

Decorate with tassels!

TIPS FOR A SUCCESSFUL PROJECT

◆ Students may want to experiment with different designs before they choose just the right one—provide extra blank graphs or graph paper.

◆ If beads are not available, you can substitute colored Lifesaver candies, cereal, or any small objects that are of equal size and have a hole in the middle.

WANT TO KEEP GOING?

◆ The beaded wall hangings students create in this activity are similar to the process of Native American beadwork. Check your local library for a book on this subject to share with your class. Choose several simple examples of beadwork patterns for students to copy on graph paper or to re-create with beads and string.

WALL HANGING PATTERN

GEOMETRY SCULPTURES

This project lets students explore the architectural possibilities of the triangle, from pyramids to geodesic domes.

WHAT YOU NEED

◆ toothpicks (multi-colored toothpicks create a wonderful effect)

◆ mini-marshmallows or gumdrops

WHAT TO DO

Student Instructions / *Teacher Notes*

1. Poke the toothpicks into the gumdrops or marshmallows. Choose the number of toothpicks you want to have in each intersection throughout your project—3, 4, or 5. Then start connecting your toothpicks and intersections.

The number of toothpicks in each intersection will determine the outcome of each sculpture—the more toothpicks, the larger and rounder the shape. Encourage students to try a variety of sculptures, or to work together to build the larger ones.

3 toothpicks
in each intersection

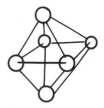

4 toothpicks
in each intersection

5 toothpicks
in each intersection.

2. **Keep building your project until you can't add any more toothpicks. Check your sculpture to make sure each intersection has the same number of toothpicks.**

Ask students if they can identify the repeating shape that adds support to their structure (triangle).

3. **Let the gumdrops or marshmallows harden overnight. Then paint your sculptures if you like.**

TIPS FOR A SUCCESSFUL PROJECT

◆ Here's a way to check that students have made their sculpture correctly:

A sculpture with 3 toothpicks in each intersection will have a total of 6 toothpicks and 4 gumdrops.

A sculpture with 6 toothpicks in each intersection will have a total of 12 toothpicks and 6 gumdrops.

A sculpture with 5 toothpicks in each intersection will have a total of 30 toothpicks and 12 gumdrops.

WANT TO KEEP GOING?

◆ Look up photos of geodesic domes in an encyclopedia. Discuss the domes together. Ask: How many supports are in each intersection of these domes?

◆ Try a larger version of this activity by replacing the toothpicks with drinking straws, and the gumdrops or mini-marshmallows with regular-sized marshmallows.

FIVE-POINTED STARS

Students will enjoy creating a whole skyful of these adorable stars while exploring decadons—ten-sided shapes.

WHAT YOU NEED

◆ rectangular construction paper or decorative paper (try metallic or day-glo)

◆ rulers

◆ scissors

WHAT TO DO

Student Instructions / *Teacher Notes*

1. Hold your paper horizontally. Fold the left side of the sheet over the right.

As they fold their stars, students can sharpen each crease by rubbing the flat side of a pencil over it.

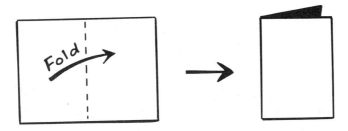

2. Use a ruler to find the exact center of the bottom edge of your folded sheet. Make a mark at that point.

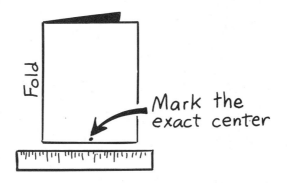

3. Fold the top-left-hand corner down so that it touches the mark.

Center
mark

4. Fold the lower-left-hand corner up over the diagonal edge of the last fold.

5. Fold the upper-right-hand corner down over the diagonal of the last fold.

6. Use your ruler to draw a diagonal line across your folded shape. Cut across the line. Unfold the shape to see your star! Make more stars and tape them to a window, or tape a piece of thread to one of the points and hang them. Either way, they make great decorations!

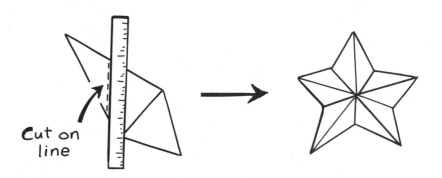

Cut on
line

TIPS FOR A SUCCESSFUL PROJECT

◆ Students may have to go through the process several times before they make a whole star—if the final diagonal cut is too low, one point of the star will be missing. Ask a student who has devised a successful method of making the last cut to share that method with the rest of the class.

◆ For an unusual effect, use paper that has a different color on each side.

WANT TO KEEP GOING?

◆ Ask students to see what will happen to their stars if they add an extra diagonal fold after step 5. (They may need to use thinner paper to do this.)

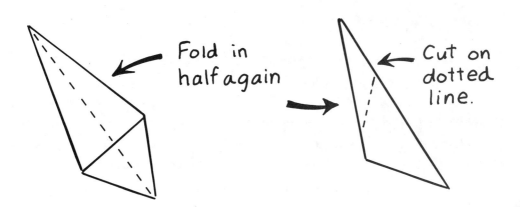

Fold in half again

Cut on dotted line.

Numbers & Computation

MATH WANTED POSTERS

These funny posters will put everyone on the lookout for math!

WHAT YOU NEED

◆ large sheets of poster paper

◆ markers or crayons

WHAT TO DO

Student Instructions / *Teacher Notes*

1. **Choose a number or a math symbol (+, −, x, or ÷) to be the subject of your Wanted poster. Describe your number or symbol on a sheet of scrap paper. You'll use these descriptions to help write your poster.**

   Here are questions students might answer to describe their numbers or symbols: What is it used for? What does it look like? When would someone need to use it? What are some math problems that use it?

2. **Begin your poster by writing the word WANTED in big letters across the top. Underneath the word, write the reason your number**

or symbol is wanted. Then draw a "mug shot" of your number or symbol and its name.

3. **Fill out the rest of your poster with some of the descriptions you wrote on your scrap paper.**

   Encourage students to use funny sentences on their posters, and to think of as many ways as possible to describe their number or symbol.

   When they have finished their posters, hang them up in your classroom or in a hallway so that others can enjoy them, too.

TIPS FOR A SUCCESSFUL PROJECT

◆ This is a project that works best with a model. Before students begin their posters, show them the photo on page 34, or create one of your own before class.

WANT TO KEEP GOING?

◆ Students may like to try creating posters for math areas (geometry, measurement, etc.), math tools (ruler, scale, calculator, etc.), or even the subject of math as a whole.

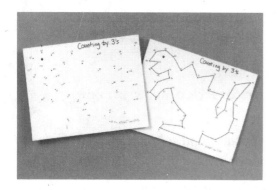

NUMBER PATTERN CONNECT-THE-DOT PUZZLES

Number patterns make solving these puzzles a challenge!

WHAT YOU NEED

◆ tracing paper or lightweight white paper

WHAT TO DO

Student Instructions / *Teacher Notes*

1. **Draw a simple picture on a sheet of lightweight paper. Try to draw an image that can be connected with one line, rather than a picture with many separate parts. Don't let anyone else see your drawing.**

You can provide artwork for students if you wish—look for simple illustrations such as those in coloring books, comic books, or on work sheets.

2. **Tape your drawing to a window that has light shining through it. Tape another sheet of paper over your drawing.**

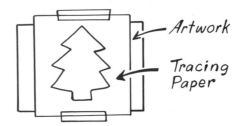

3. **Begin marking dots around the edge of your drawing. Label the first dot START. But instead of numbering the dots 1, 2, 3, and so on, number them in a pattern. Figure out your pattern before you number all of your dots. Write the name of your pattern above the dots.**

There are many number patterns students can use to number their dots. Suggest counting by twos, fives, or tens, or using an arithmetic pattern such as "plus 1, plus 2; plus 1, plus 2; etc."

Counting by 5's

4. **Exchange finished dot drawings with another student. See if he or she can follow your pattern to make your original picture again.**

   If students have made any mistakes numbering their dots, this is when they'll find out about it! If any student is trying to solve a puzzle and thinks that it may include a numbering error, he or she should give it back to the artist and ask for it to be checked over and corrected, if necessary.

TIPS FOR A SUCCESSFUL PROJECT

◆ Students should try not to use so many dots that the picture is apparent without even connecting them (but they should use enough dots to create a recognizable picture after they are connected).

WANT TO KEEP GOING?

◆ Have students try these funny "backward" dot-to-dot puzzles: Cover a page with about 30 dots. Label one dot START, then number the rest of the dots randomly, using a number pattern. Connect the dots in the order of the number pattern, and see what kind of design comes up. Make up a funny name to describe what the picture looks like.

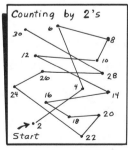

A Broken Kite!

5 × 4 = 20

MULTIPLICATION CONSTELLATIONS

Here's an "out of this world" project that will help your students visualize the meaning of multiplication.

WHAT YOU NEED

◆ new or old kitchen sponges

◆ large pieces of black or dark blue construction paper

◆ white, yellow, or metallic silver or gold poster paint

◆ white or metallic crayons

◆ paint dishes (plastic "clamshell" containers cut in half work well)

◆ old newspapers

WHAT TO DO

Student Instructions / *Teacher Notes*

1. *Prepare for this activity by cutting the kitchen sponges into small star shapes (about one to two inches across). Give one star sponge to each student. Spread out old newspapers on the work area and pour a small amount of poster paint into the paint dishes.*

2. Choose a multiplication problem, such as "4 x 5." Or wait for your teacher to give you a multiplication problem or a product.

Gear the multiplication level of this activity to students' abilities. If they're just starting to learn about multiplication, assign them problems such as "2 x 3" or "3 x 4." If the multiplication table is old hat to students, give them just a product, such as 72, and let them create as many constellations as possible that fit that product.

3. Dip your star sponge in the paint. Wipe off any excess paint against the side of the paint dish. Draw your multiplication problem as a constellation by making rows of stars on the construction paper. Each row in the constellation must have the same number of stars.

The constellation for "4 x 5" would look like this:

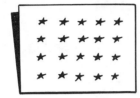

The constellation for "5 x 4" would look like this:

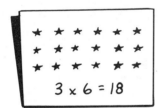

4. Use a crayon to write the multiplication problem and its solution under the constellation.

TIPS FOR A SUCCESSFUL PROJECT

◆ To keep spills at a minimum, refill the paint dishes only when necessary, and don't fill them more than 1/2-inch deep each time. Encourage students to plan out each constellation with pencil dots on their construction paper before they start putting down stars. That will save them frustration (and save paint and paper).

WANT TO KEEP GOING?

◆ Work on this project several times until students have created a constellation for every multiplication problem from "1 x 1" to "12 x 12." Display the constellations on your classroom ceiling, creating an entire multiplication sky!

MULTIPLICATION HOUSES

These little houses are a fun way for students to practice their multiplication tables—and they're fun to make, too!

WHAT YOU NEED

◆ two sheets of construction paper (in two colors) for each house

◆ crayons

◆ scissors

◆ stapler

WHAT TO DO

Student Instructions / *Teacher Notes*

1. Choose one sheet of construction paper to be the front of your house. Draw a big house on the sheet with crayons. Make sure your house includes a front door and 13 windows. The windows can be anywhere on the house as long as they don't touch an edge of the paper.

Label each window

2. Label each window with a number from 0 to 12. Then decide which multiplication table will "live" in your house. Write the name of the multiplication table on the front door. For example, if you choose the fives table, write HOUSE OF FIVES or THE FIVES' HOUSE on the door.

3. **Carefully cut each window along any three sides. Now your windows can open and close!**

Students may need help cutting out the windows.

Cut on three sides only

4. **Staple your house to the other sheet of construction paper. Open each window and write the answer to the multiplication problem formed by the door and the front of the window. For example, in the House of Fives, the "3" window will need the answer 15 behind it (5 x 3).**

Students may need to consult a multiplication table to make sure they have the correct number behind each window.

5. **After you have written the correct answer behind all 13 windows, use your house to test some multiplication facts on yourself or a friend!**

TIPS FOR A SUCCESSFUL PROJECT

◆ Create and display your own sample house before students begin making theirs.

WANT TO KEEP GOING?

◆ Work together to create a house for every multiplication table. Start with the House of Ones and finish with the House of Twelves. You'll have a whole multiplication neighborhood! Place the houses in a math center for students to use as a resource.

◆ Students can also try making addition houses, subtraction houses, and division houses.

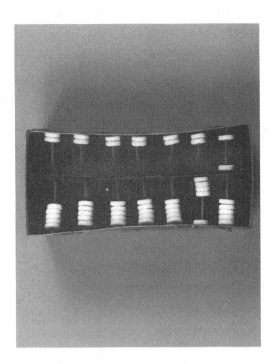

MAKE AN ABACUS

These ancient calculators can really help your students understand how place value works.

WHAT YOU NEED

◆ empty shoe box (or any box of a similar shape)

◆ 1-inch-wide strip of cardboard or heavy paper, the same length as the shoe box

◆ string or yarn

◆ beads that will fit on the string or yarn (you'll need seven beads for each place on the abacus)

◆ hole-punch

◆ scissors

WHAT TO DO

Student Instructions / *Teacher Notes*

1. **Punch seven holes in the top and in the bottom of your shoe box. Line up the holes as best you can. Label the bottom holes from "millions" down to "ones."**

These directions are for an abacus that goes up to the millions place. You may want students to use fewer places (therefore, they'll need fewer holes). They may also need your help in labeling the holes.

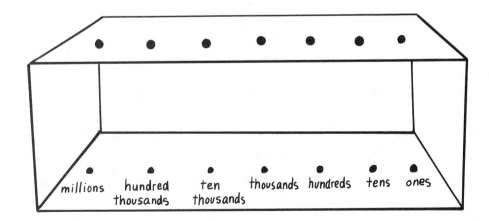

2. Cut off a length of string that is about six feet long. Thread the string through the lower-right-hand hole of your box. Tape the end of the string to the bottom of the box.

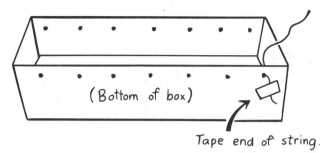

(Bottom of box)

Tape end of string.

3. Place seven beads onto the string, and pass the string through the upper-right-hand hole in the box.

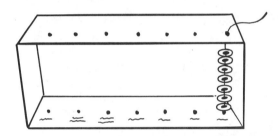

4. Thread the string into the next hole to the left. Place seven more beads on the string, and pass the string out the bottom hole.

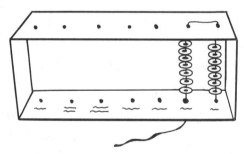

5. String seven beads for each set of holes in your box. When you get to the last hole, tape the end of the string and cut off the excess.

Tape end.

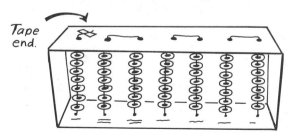

6. Hold your cardboard strip against the strings along the inside bottom of your box. Draw a straight line where each string hits the cardboard. Then cut along each line, but don't cut all the way across the strip.

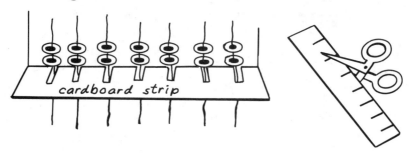

7. Slide the strings into each slot on the cardboard strip. Be sure that two beads are above the strip on each string, and five beads are below it. Tape the ends of the strip to the box. Your abacus is complete!

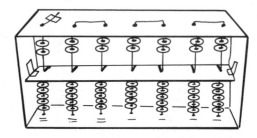

TIPS FOR A SUCCESSFUL PROJECT

◆ You'll probably want to stay with students throughout each procedure on this project, since there are so many. (However, any mistakes on this project are easy to remedy.) Try to keep the strings on each abacus taut, but not overly tight.

◆ Instead of beads, you can substitute Lifesaver candies (Pep-o-mint flavor works well because the candies don't stick together) or any small objects that are of equal size and can be threaded on the string.

WANT TO KEEP GOING?

◆ Give students the opportunity to use their abaci by challenging them to create numbers and solve addition problems. (See page 45.)

◆ Have students look up the abacus in an encyclopedia to learn its history. They may be surprised to find out that many people still use an abacus every day.

HOW TO USE AN ABACUS

Each string on the abacus (from right to left) stands for a place from ones to millions. The beads below the center bar stand for one unit, and the beads above the bar stand for five units. The most you can show in any place is nine units; any higher and you must move a place to the left. The "start" position for the abacus has all of the beads pushed away from the bar.

To create a number on the abacus, push the necessary beads toward the center bar. This abacus shows the number 349:

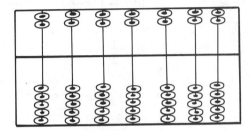

3 hundreds
4 tens
5+4=9 ones

To solve an addition problem, set the beads up to show the first number. Then add the second number place by place, starting with the ones. Every time five "ones" beads are moved to the center bar, move a "five" bead to the bar and push the "ones" back down. Every time two "fives" beads are moved to the center bar, shift one place to the left, move a "ones" bead to the bar and move the "fives" back down.

Here's how to do the problem 26 + 19:

1. 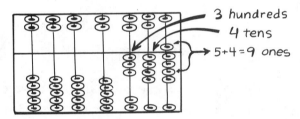 26

2. 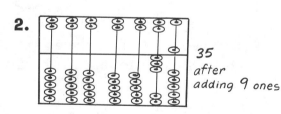 35 after adding 9 ones

3. 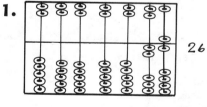 45 after adding 1 ten

PLACE VALUE SNAKES

These silly snakes provide a hiss-terical way for students to explore place value!

WHAT YOU NEED

◆ empty egg carton for each student

◆ glue

◆ markers

◆ stapler

◆ small counters of any kind

◆ arts-and-crafts materials for decorating ("googly" eyes, sequins, pipe cleaners, felt)

WHAT TO DO

Student Instructions / *Teacher Notes*

1. Cut the lid off of the egg carton. Cut the base of the egg carton down the middle, so that you have two rows of six holes.)

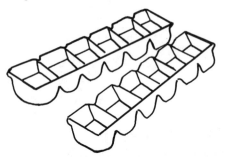

2. Cut two holes off of one end of a row of six. Staple these two holes to the other row, so that you have a row of eight holes.

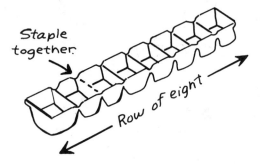

Staple together.

Row of eight

3. Cut off one more hole from the short row. Glue it on top of the first hole in your long row. This will be the head of your snake. Decorate the head with eyes and a tongue.

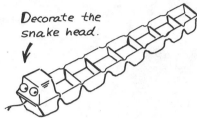

Decorate the snake head.

4. Label the holes of your snake from "millions" all the way down to "ones" with a marker. If you like, decorate your place value snake!

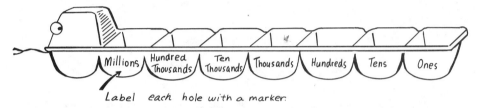

Millions Hundred Thousands Ten Thousands Thousands Hundreds Tens Ones

Label each hole with a marker.

5. Your place value snake is finished. Here's how it works: Each counter you drop into a snake's hole stands for one unit in that place. For example, two counters in the "tens" hole stands for two tens, or 20. Here's what the number 6,035 would look like:

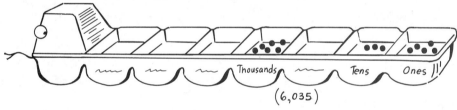

Thousands   Tens   Ones

(6,035)

Give students some sample numbers to make with the snakes and counters.

TIPS FOR A SUCCESSFUL PROJECT

◆ Allow enough time for the glue holding the two parts of the snake's head together to dry.

WANT TO KEEP GOING?

◆ Ask: What's the highest number of counters that can ever be in one of the snake's holes? (nine) Why?

◆ These snakes can, of course, represent places higher than millions—have students construct a 13-hole snake that goes all the way to trillions!

Mutiples of 5

NUMBER COLLAGES

Numbers alone are the focus of these works of art!

WHAT YOU NEED

◆ old magazines and newspapers

◆ construction paper or oak tag

◆ glue

WHAT TO DO

Student Instructions / *Teacher Notes*

1. Look through the magazines and newspapers for the types of numbers your teacher tells you to find.

Students can simply look for "numbers ending in 5" or "two-digit numbers." For a more challenging search, students can hunt for more complicated numbers such as "numbers that are divisible by 3" or "decimal numbers." Encourage students to include numbers written in words, as well as in digits, in their collages.

2. Your collage will look more interesting if you cut out some of the numbers and rip out others. It's okay if you include some of the page around each number.

Cut out

Ripped out

3. As you gather your numbers, start gluing them to your sheet of construction paper or oak tag. Overlap the edges of the numbers so that none of the background shows through. If you can't find enough

numbers in the magazines and newspapers, draw some of your own and add them to your collage.

4. After your collage is completely covered with numbers, add a title to it.

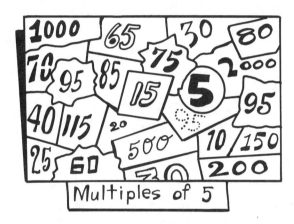

TIPS FOR A SUCCESSFUL PROJECT

◆ A few weeks before you begin this project, ask students to bring in periodicals that can be cut up. Some types of magazines and newspapers, such as those that deal with business and finance, are more likely to contain numbers.

◆ Let students work on this project over several days to give them adequate time to search for their numbers.

WANT TO KEEP GOING?

◆ Form a "supercollage" on a bulletin board by pinning up students' collages without any spaces in beween.

Measurement

ONE-METER DESIGNS

You'll be surprised to see how creative students can be with just one meter!

WHAT YOU NEED

◆ string or yarn

◆ metersticks

◆ construction paper

◆ glue (try using school glue that comes in different colors)

WHAT TO DO

Student Instructions / *Teacher Notes*

1. Measure out one meter of string with the meterstick. Cut off the string.

If students are new to the metric system, spend a few minutes talking about meters. Ask: Are you taller or shorter than one meter? What can you think of that's about one meter wide? Do you know any other measurement words that contain the word "meter"? (centimeter, millimeter, kilometer, etc.)

2. Lay the string on your construction paper. Move the string around to create a picture. You must use the whole length of string in your picture.

Here are some picture ideas to get students started:

3. **After you have decided on a picture, glue your string down in that shape.**

   Display the pictures together so that everyone can see how many different ways a line of the same length can appear.

TIPS FOR A SUCCESSFUL PROJECT

◆ If you're using a clear-drying glue, you might try squeezing some of the glue out into a paint dish and letting students dip their entire length of string into the glue. Then they can just leave the string in place on the construction paper rather than spot gluing it.

WANT TO KEEP GOING?

◆ Have students try to draw a one-meter design with a crayon. They can check the length of their designs by tracing them with a one-meter string. See how closely they can guess the lengths before they check them.

MAGIC FOLDING CUBES

Students measure and cut three strips of paper, then learn the secret way to fold them into a cube.

WHAT YOU NEED

◆ Cube Ruler for each student (reproducible page 54)

◆ square or rectangular sheets of construction paper that are at least 10-by-6 inches wide

◆ scissors

WHAT TO DO

Student Instructions / *Teacher Notes*

1. **Cut out your Cube Ruler along the solid lines.**

2. **Use the arrows on the Cube Ruler to help you measure three strips on your sheet of construction paper. Each strip must be 10 inches long and 2 inches wide. Be sure to begin measuring the paper from two straight sides.**

If necessary, check students' measurements before they go on to the next step.

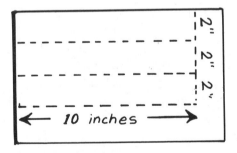

3. **Cut out the three strips. Use the Cube Ruler again to measure and draw four lines on each strip. The lines must be 2 inches apart.**

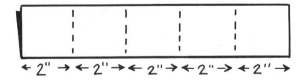

4. Make a crease along each line on the strips. You can make the creases sharper by rubbing them with the flat side of a pencil.

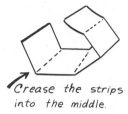

Crease the strips into the middle.

5. Here's the secret trick to turning the three strips into a cube: Start by folding one strip into a square. One end will overlap the other end.

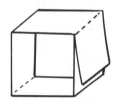

6. Wrap another strip around the first one, and tuck the two ends inside.

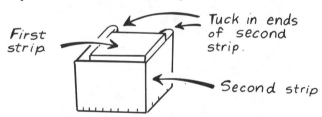

First strip

Tuck in ends of second strip.

Second strip

7. Now wrap the third strip around the open end of the box. Tuck the two ends into the back. The two ends will overlap each other. Practice making the cube until you can do it easily. Then challenge your friends and family to try it!

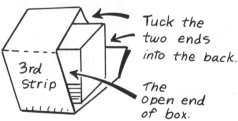

3rd Strip

Tuck the two ends into the back.

The open end of box.

TIPS FOR A SUCCESSFUL PROJECT

◆ You may need to demonstrate the cube-making process a few times for students before they get the knack. If somebody's cube isn't quite fitting together the right way, ask him or her to check the strips to see if they are measured correctly.

CUBE RULER

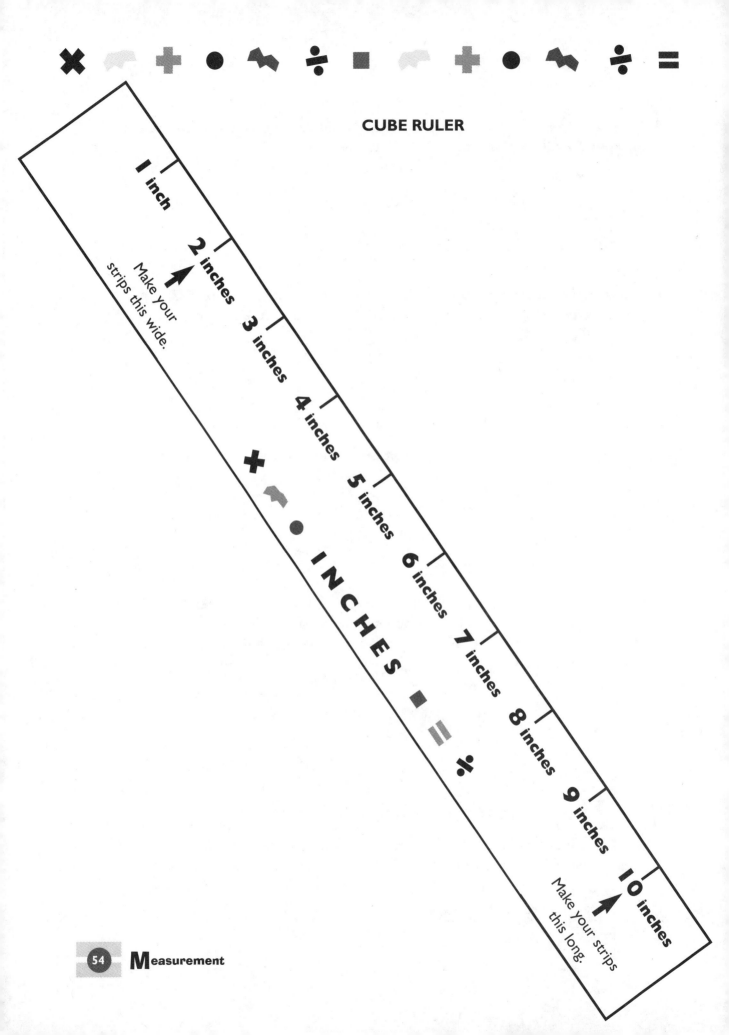

1 inch

Make your
strips this wide.

2 inches

3 inches

4 inches

5 inches

6 inches

INCHES

7 inches

8 inches

9 inches

Make your strips
this long.

10 inches

PERPETUAL CALENDARS

Making a perpetual calendar will help students explore the cycle of days, months, and years.

WHAT YOU NEED

◆ Perpetual Calendar Pieces for each student (reproducible page 58)

◆ 8½-by-11-inch sheet of colored oak tag for each student

◆ twelve 1-by-3-inch strips of oak tag or stiff paper for each student

◆ Velcro tape

◆ rulers marked in inches

◆ oak tag in sheets

◆ scissors

◆ envelopes

◆ tape

◆ ribbon

◆ hole-punch

WHAT TO DO

Student Instructions / *Teacher Notes*

1. **Glue the sheet of calendar pieces to a sheet of oak tag. Let the glue dry, then cut out the calendar pieces.**

2. **Make a pencil mark three inches down on each side of the colored oak tag. Connect the dots with a light pencil line.**

3. Make a dot on the pencil line 1½ inches in from each side.

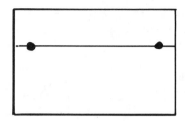

4. Glue or stick a strip of Velcro tape (the fuzzy side) under the pencil line. The Velcro tape should fit just inside the two dots on the pencil line.

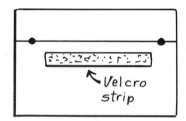

↖ Velcro
strip

5. Glue or tape a 1-inch strip of Velcro tape (the side with the hooks) to the back of each calendar piece. The tape should start just below the top of each piece.

6. Stick any seven calendar pieces on the calendar, using the Velcro tape. Line up the tops of the pieces. Write the word SUNDAY above the first piece. Write the word MONDAY over the second piece. Keep labeling the pieces until you get to SATURDAY.

Sun.	Mon.	Tue.	Wed.	Thu.	Fri.	Sat.
1	2	3	4	5	6	7
8	9	10	11	12	13	14
15	16	17	18	19	20	21
22	23	24	25	26	27	28

7. **Glue or tape a 2-inch strip of Velcro tape (the fuzzy side) above the days of the week.**

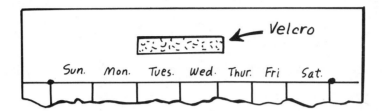

8. **Label each oak tag strip with a month of the year, from January all the way to December. Glue or tape a 2-inch strip of Velcro tape (the side with the hooks) to the back of each month.**

You may have to write the names of the months on the chalkboard for students' reference.

9. **Match your perpetual calendar to this month's calendar. You'll be able to rearrange your calendar and use it again every month, forever!**

TIPS FOR A SUCCESSFUL PROJECT

◆ To finish the calendar off as a gift: Have students decorate it, then punch two holes at the top of the calendar and string a ribbon through as a hanger. Store the unused month and day pieces in an envelope taped to the back of the calendar.

PERPETUAL CALENDAR PIECES

6	13	20	27	2	1
5	12	19	26	9	8
4	11	18	25	16	15
3	10	17	24	23	22
2	9	16	23	30	7
3	10	17	24	31	14
1	8	15	22	29	21
					28

LIFETIME TIME LINES

In this activity, students use inches and feet to conceptualize and document the months and years of their lives.

WHAT YOU NEED

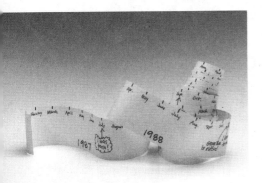

◆ adding-machine tape

◆ rulers marked in inches

◆ crayons or markers

WHAT TO DO

Student Instructions / *Teacher Notes*

1. **Measure out one foot of adding-machine tape for each calendar year you have been alive (include this year, too). Cut the tape to the correct length.**

Students might need your help in figuring out the right length. If most of your students were born during the same year, they'll all need the same length. All students' lengths of tape should be a whole number of feet long—regardless of the month in which they were born, or what the current month is.

2. **Measure and draw a line at every foot on the tape. Label the first foot with the year you were born. Continue labeling the tape up to this year.**

1987	1988	1989	1990	1991	1992	1993	1994	1995	1996

1 Foot

3. **Now make a mark at every inch between the foot marks. Start labeling the marks with January and continue up to December of the present year. You can abbreviate each month's name if you like.**

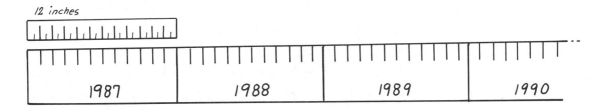

12 inches

1987	1988	1989	1990

4. Go back to the first month on the tape. Draw an arrow to the month you were born. Record the date and a comment such as, "I was born!" Draw a picture of yourself as a baby in the same spot.

5. Record other important dates in your life in the correct spots on the time line.

Some of the events that might be included on a time line: the date a younger brother or sister was born, the first day of school, each year's birthday, a pet's birthday, a special vacation trip, a move to a new home, etc. Students may need their parents' help in determining some of the dates. You can help everyone include important world events on their time lines as well (e.g., "Bill Clinton elected president," "Berlin Wall comes down").

Encourage students to decorate their time lines with illustrations of the events they have detailed. They can also attach photographs to their time lines.

TIPS FOR A SUCCESSFUL PROJECT

◆ Ask students to discuss and write down the dates of their important life events with their parents before you do this activity.

WANT TO KEEP GOING?

◆ Students can always add more tape to their time lines as time passes so they can continue to document their lives.

◆ Here's a rich and meaningful project for students to work on with a grandparent or an older relative: Have students measure out two inches of tape for every year of the person's life. They'll mark off every two inches of the tape and label each space with a year. Then the student and the relative can work together to fill the years with the relative's important life events.

MARVELOUS MOBILES

Students explore weights and balancing points as they create mobiles that really work!

WHAT YOU NEED

- ◆ heavyweight thread (such as button-and-carpet thread)
- ◆ two thin dowels or sticks, one about ten inches long and one about seven inches long, for each student
- ◆ variety of small objects to hang on the mobiles such as beads, buttons, shells, etc.

WHAT TO DO

Student Instructions / *Teacher Notes*

1. **Begin with the short dowel. Choose two objects that are about the same weight. Tie a 12-inch length of thread through each object. Let the objects hang about six inches down from the dowel, then tightly tie the other ends of the thread to the ends of the dowel. Leave about one inch at each end of the dowel.**

   For a more colorful look, students can paint the dowels before they put the mobiles together.

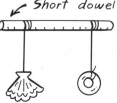

2. **Cut another 12-inch length of thread and tie one end to the middle of your dowel. Tie the thread tight enough so that the dowel doesn't slide around, but loose enough that you can adjust the dowel a bit. Hold the string in one hand and shift the dowel in the knot from side to side until the two weights balance.**

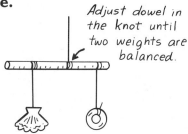

3. Tie your balanced weights tightly to the longer dowel. Let the short dowel hang down about six inches from the longer dowel. Leave about an inch at the end of the long dowel.

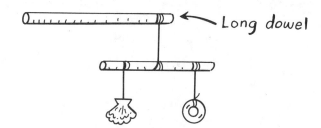

4. Choose another object that weighs about the same as your first two objects put together. Cut a two-foot length of thread and tie it to the object. Let the new object hang as short or as long as you want, then tie the other end of the thread tightly to the open end of the long dowel. Leave about an inch at the end of the dowel.

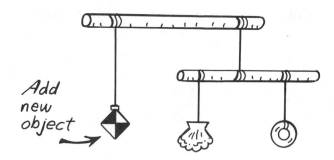

Add new object →

5. Repeat step 2 for the long dowel. Adjust the dowel until the whole mobile balances.

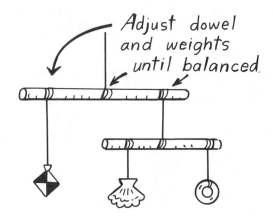

Adjust dowel and weights until balanced.

TIPS FOR A SUCCESSFUL PROJECT

◆ The trickiest part of this project is in tying the "balancing threads" at the proper tightness so that the dowels can be adjusted. Here's an idea that may help students: Have them wrap a rubber band around the middle of each dowel before they tie objects on it. When they're ready to balance the dowel, they can slip the balancing thread through the rubber band. They can then shift the dowel from side to side without it slipping.

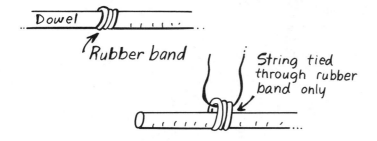

WANT TO KEEP GOING?

◆ Students can add one more level to their mobiles by repeating steps 4 and 5 with a longer dowel and a heavier object.

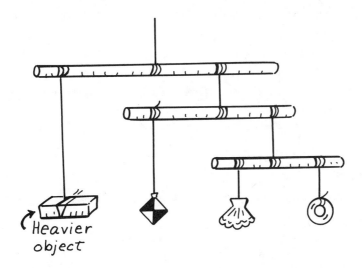

◆ American artist Alexander Calder is well known for his mobile sculptures. Look for books on Calder in your library and share his work with students.

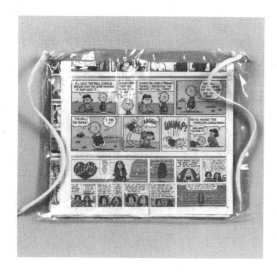

SIT-UPONS

Students use their measurement skills to make a dirt-proof and waterproof take-along seat.

WHAT YOU NEED

◆ old magazine (the larger, the better) or a tabloid-sized newspaper for each student

◆ stapler

◆ old or new plastic shower-curtain liners—solid color, patterned, or clear (about one shower curtain for every eight students)

◆ yardsticks, metersticks, or measuring tapes

◆ hole-punch

◆ long shoelace for each student

◆ waterproof paints or permanent markers

WHAT TO DO

Student Instructions / *Teacher Notes*

1. Measure the width and height of your magazine.

Decide whether students will do their measuring in inches or in centimeters.

2. You will need to cut a rectangular section of the shower curtain that is the following size:

the height of your magazine plus two inches
and
twice the width of your magazine plus two inches

Figure out your dimensions on paper before you begin to measure the shower curtain.

Substitute "six centimeters" for "two inches" if you're working in metrics.

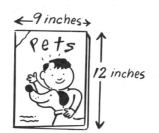

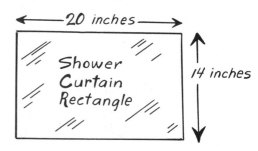

3. Start measuring the shower curtain (it's easier to measure your rectangle if you start at a straight edge or a corner). Use a ballpoint pen or a permanent marker to mark off your rectangle.

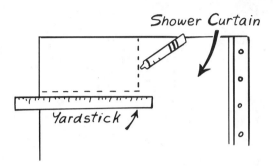

Shower Curtain

Yardstick ↑

4. Cut out the rectangle and wrap it around your magazine. Staple the three open sides together.

Pets

← *Staple on three sides*

5. Punch a hole in each upper corner of your "sit-upon." Cut the shoelace in half, and tie and knot each half through one of the holes. If you like, decorate your sit-upon with waterproof paints or markers.

6. Tie your sit-upon around your waist. It's ready for you to sit upon!

TIPS FOR A SUCCESSFUL PROJECT

◆ The old adage "measure twice, cut once" applies to this project as well. Make sure students remeasure the lines they have drawn on their shower curtain sections before they cut them out.

◆ If you use clear shower-curtain liners, students can wrap and tape their own paintings or drawings around the magazine before stapling. Then their personal artwork will show through their sit-upons!

WANT TO KEEP GOING?

◆ Now that students are equipped with sit-upons, go on a math hike! The hike can take place anywhere from a neighborhood park to your own school yard. Along the way, challenge students to be on the lookout for math sightings such as numbers, geometric shapes, patterns, symmetry, lines, angles, and people using math on the job.

Patterns

TERRIFIC TESSELLATIONS

These beautiful repeating designs are easy to create and fun to look at.

WHAT YOU NEED

◆ Tessellation Patterns for each student (reproducible page 70)

◆ lightweight cardboard

◆ scissors

◆ light-colored construction paper

◆ crayons, paint, or markers

WHAT TO DO

Student Instructions / *Teacher Notes*

1. **Choose one of the tessellation patterns and cut it out. Trace the pattern onto the lightweight cardboard, and cut out the shape.**

If students are not familiar with the term, explain that a "tessellation" is a design that repeats over and over.

2. **Trace the outline of your cardboard shape anywhere on the construction paper. Use a pencil that has a sharp point.**

If students use too thick a line to trace their shapes, the tracings may not all match up.

3. Slide your shape in any direction (don't flip it or turn it) until two of the sides match up. Then trace the shape again.

4. Slide and trace your shape until the whole page is full. Now color in your tessellation. If you think your shape looks like an animal, a person, or an object, decorate your tessellation to highlight your shape's features.

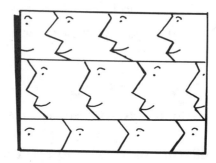

TIPS FOR A SUCCESSFUL PROJECT

◆ Students should try to trace around the edges of their cardboard shapes as closely as possible. They will not need to redraw the lines of any shared sides between two shapes.

WANT TO KEEP GOING?

◆ Dutch artist M.C. Escher is famous for his fascinating and intricate tessellation designs. Look in your library for some examples of Escher's work to examine and discuss with your class. (Educational-supply companies, such as Dale Seymour, also offer books and posters of Escher's work in their catalogs.)

◆ Ask: What are some examples of tessellations that we see every day? Answers might include: tiled walls and floors, designs on fabric and clothing, bricks on buildings and patios, etc.

◆ Students can create their own tessellation patterns. Here's how:

1. Draw any design on one side of a square piece of cardboard. The design should start and end on the same side, and should not touch any other side.

2. Cut out the design in one piece. Slide the piece directly to the opposite side, and tape the pieces together along the two straight sides.

3. Repeat steps 1 and 2 with the top and bottom of the square. The shape is ready to tessellate.

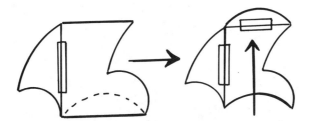

TESSELLATION PATTERNS

WEAVE A NUMBER PATTERN

What does a number pattern look like? These woven designs will give students a chance to find out!

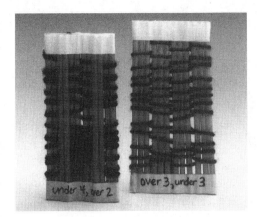

under 4, over 2   over 3, under 3

WHAT YOU NEED

◆ 12 plastic drinking straws for each student

◆ masking tape or colorful plastic tape

◆ yarn or colored string

WHAT TO DO

Student Instructions / *Teacher Notes*

1. **Lay a strip of masking tape about 12 inches long on your desk, sticky-side-up. Line up the ends of the straws and lay them on the masking tape. Leave a bit of space between them.**

Masking tape, sticky side up.

2. **Wrap the ends of the tape around the front of your straws. Add more tape if you need it. Tape one end of the yarn right near the bottom of the first straw.**

Masking tape

3. **Choose a number pattern and weave it from left to right.**

Here are the number patterns that will work best on 12 straws. As variations, students can switch the order of the numbers in each pair or the "under" and "over" of each pair.

over 5, under 1	*over 2, under 1*	*over 3, under 3*
over 2, under 2	*under 3, over 3*	*under 4, over 2*
under 4, over 4	*under 6, over 6*	*over 3, under 1*

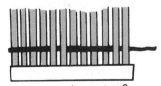

over 4, under 2

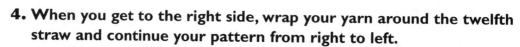

4. When you get to the right side, wrap your yarn around the twelfth straw and continue your pattern from right to left.

The twelfth straw in one direction will become the first straw in the opposite direction.

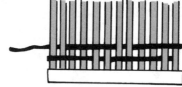

5. Keep on weaving your pattern. If you run out of yarn or if you want to switch yarn colors, just tie on more yarn.

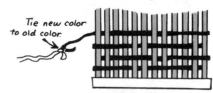

Tie new color to old color.

6. When you have almost reached the tops of the straws, finish a row and tie your string to the end straw. Then tape the tops of your straws together. Tie a short length of string to the top as a hanger. Label your weaving with the name of the pattern you used.

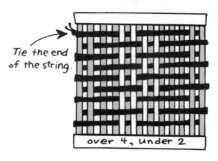

Tie the end of the string.

over 4, under 2

TIPS FOR A SUCCESSFUL PROJECT

◆ If a student's weaving doesn't start to show a visible pattern, he or she may have made a counting mistake. Examine the pattern with the student until you find the place where he or she went astray. Then unwind the yarn to that point and begin the weaving again.

WANT TO KEEP GOING?

◆ Bring a woven rug or a woven basket into class and let students take a closer look at the patterns it contains.

◆ Let students try weaving on a real loom.

NUMBER SPIRALS

Round and round go these graceful patterns of numbers and lines!

WHAT YOU NEED

◆ Number Spirals Circle for each student (reproducible page 75)

◆ rulers

◆ fine-tipped markers or colored pencils with sharp points

WHAT TO DO

Student Instructions / *Teacher Notes*

1. Begin at the star at the top of the circle. Choose a number from 2 to 9. Move clockwise that many dots around the circle. (If you chose the number 4, you would stop on dot 4.)

Students may want to keep track of each new dot by placing a counter on or near it.

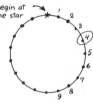

2. Use your ruler and a fine-tipped marker to draw a line from the star to the new dot.

3. Move clockwise again around the circle, counting out your chosen number of dots. (If you chose the number 4, you would now stop at dot 8.) Connect the end of your last line to the new dot.

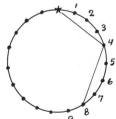

4. Keep counting dots and drawing lines until you reach the star again. You will create a beautiful spiral pattern. Cut out the circle and hang up your spiral design.

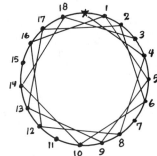

5. Choose another number from 2 to 9, and make a new spiral on a blank circle. Or draw the second spiral right over the first one in a different color.

Ask: How does the shape of the spiral change as the number you choose gets larger? (The larger the number, the "pointier" the spiral.) Have you found a strategy for drawing the spirals without having to keep on counting dots? (A pattern begins to emerge as students connect the dots.)

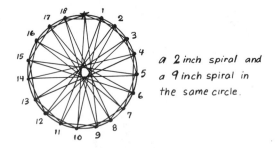

a 2 inch spiral and a 9 inch spiral in the same circle.

TIPS FOR A SUCCESSFUL PROJECT

◆ Students need to be precise about counting the dots and drawing the lines, or the spirals will not work out correctly. (Watch for spirals that come back to the star but contain unconnected dots, or spirals that start to repeat the same lines again—both situations indicate miscounted dots or misdrawn lines.)

WANT TO KEEP GOING?

◆ You and your students can construct a more permanent version of this activity by taping a blank spiral circle to a block of wood, hammering a small nail through each dot, then removing the paper. Wrap colored string or yarn from nail to nail.

NUMBER SPIRALS CIRCLE

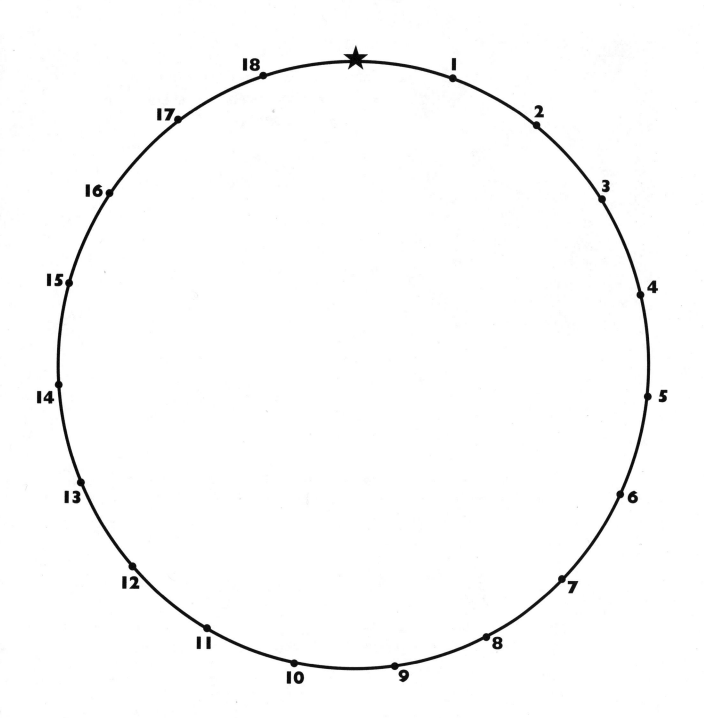

STATISTICS

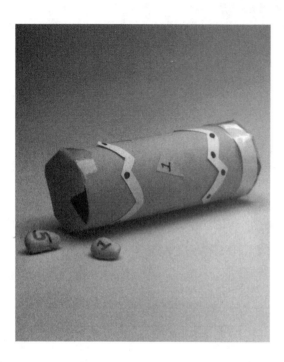

NUMBER SHAKERS

These fun shakers will come in handy for exploring probability or for generating random numbers for board games.

WHAT YOU NEED

◆ paper-towel tube or toilet-paper tube for each student

◆ construction paper

◆ permanent marker

◆ crayons or markers

◆ tape

◆ beans, buttons, pennies, or other inexpensive counters

◆ scissors

WHAT TO DO

Student Instructions / *Teacher Notes*

1. Tape one edge of a sheet of construction paper to your tube. Roll the tube inside the paper, cut off the excess, and tape it all along the open edge.

Roll the construction paper around the tube.

2. Trace one end of your tube twice on scraps of construction paper. Cut out the circles. Tape one circle tightly to one end of your tube.

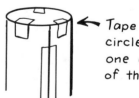

Tape one circle to one end of the tube.

3. Count out and label your counters with a permanent marker. You may want to number them on both sides.

Choose the number of counters you wish your students to use in their shakers. To use a shaker as one die, label six counters from 1 to 6. To use a shaker as a pair of dice, label 12 counters from 1 to 6 twice. To use the shaker for board games, label four counters from 1 to 4.

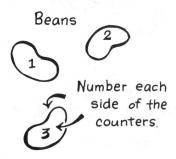

Beans

Number each side of the counters.

4. Cut a small wedge in your remaining circle. Hold it against the open end of your tube to see if one counter will fit through it. Increase the size of the wedge until the counter slides through easily without too much extra space. Tape the circle to the tube. Don't tape over the open wedge!

Make sure your counters can fit through the wedge!

5. Slip your counters through the wedge. Decorate your shaker with numbers and designs.

6. **To use your number shaker, shake it gently from side to side until one counter comes out of the hole. Put the counter back inside before you shake your shaker again!**

TIPS FOR A SUCCESSFUL PROJECT

◆ You may want to use stiffer paper for the ends of the shakers and attach them with stronger tape, especially if you're using heavier counters such as pennies.

WANT TO KEEP GOING?

◆ Here's a probability game your students can play if their shakers contain 12 counters numbered twice from 1 to 6:

Play in groups of three or four. The group can share one number shaker, or each player can use his or her own shaker. Each player chooses two different numbers from 2 to 12. Players take turns shaking out two counters and adding them together. Each time the sum tuns out to be a player's chosen number, he or she gets one point. The game continues until one player gets ten points.

After your students have played the game a number of times, ask: Which numbers between 2 and 12 seemed to come up more often? Did any of the numbers hardly seem to come up at all? Which numbers are most likely to come up? Why do you think so? (The numbers 6, 7, 8, and 9 are more likely to come up because they can be formed the most ways with two counters. The numbers 2 and 12 are least likely to come up because they can each only be made one way—two 1's or two 6's.)

FAMILY GARDEN BAR GRAPH

These springtime bar graphs make perfect Mother's Day, Father's Day or Grandparents' Day gifts.

WHAT YOU NEED

◆ Family Garden Bar Graph for each student (reproducible page 81)

◆ construction paper

◆ glue

◆ scissors

◆ crayons or markers

◆ each student will also need to bring in a small photograph of each of his or her family members that can be cut up

◆ tape measures or measuring sticks

WHAT TO DO

Student Instructions / *Teacher Notes*

1. **Measure the height of each person in your family. You can do this by having each person stand up straight inside a doorway. Place a book on the person's head, line up the back of the book against the doorway, and make a tiny pencil mark at the bottom of the book. Then measure from the pencil mark to the floor with a tape measure or measuring stick.**

2. **Cut out the blank graph along the dotted lines. Glue the graph in the center of a sheet of construction paper. Write the name of each person in your family under the graph. (Don't forget to include yourself!)**

The names need not be in any order, but some students may prefer to list their family members by age or by height. For students with large families, tape two graphs together.

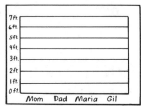

3. **Draw a flower on the graph above each person's name. The very top of each flower should reach the person's height on the graph.**

Students may need your help in drawing their flowers in the correct spot.

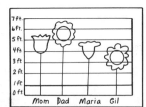

Note: *In the photo on page 79, each person's face, not the flower, reaches his or her height on the graph.*

4. **Cut out each family member's face from the photos. Glue each person's face to his or her flower. Give your graph a title. Then decorate the whole page to look like a garden.**

TIPS FOR A SUCCESSFUL PROJECT

◆ If it's not possible for students to bring in photos, they can draw pictures of the faces of each family member.

◆ Instead of family graphs, students can make graphs that include friends, neighbors, and pets!

◆ You may need to review measuring in inches and feet, and/or reading a bar graph, before you begin this activity.

WANT TO KEEP GOING?

◆ Create a Classroom Garden bar graph, including all students. (A great time to do this is right after they receive their school pictures.)

FAMILY GARDEN BAR GRAPH

7 feet	6 feet	5 feet	4 feet	3 feet	2 feet	1 feet	0 feet

FRACTIONS

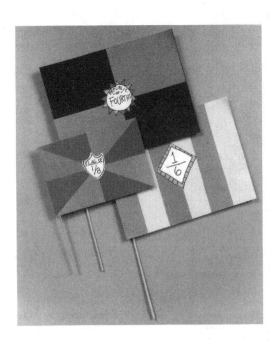

FRACTION FLAGS

These colorful banners will help your students stand up and salute fractions!

WHAT YOU NEED

◆ rectangular sheets of construction paper in light or medium shades

◆ crayons or markers

◆ pencils

◆ glue

◆ tape

◆ rulers

◆ straws, wooden skewers, or dowels for the "flagpoles"

WHAT TO DO
Student Instructions / *Teacher Notes*

1. Using a pencil and ruler, divide a sheet of construction paper into fractions. There are lots of different fractions you can draw.

Remind students that each fraction of the construction paper should be the same size and shape. Here are some ways students can divide the paper into fractions:

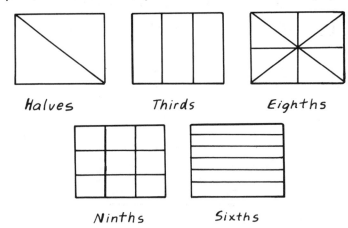

Halves   Thirds   Eighths

Ninths   Sixths

2. After you have divided your paper into fractions, color each fraction a different color.

3. On another sheet of paper, draw a "seal" for your flag. Include your chosen fraction on the seal.

Below are some ideas for flag seals. Students can also use an almanac or encyclopedia to look at pictures of real flags to see other types of seals.

4. Glue the seal to your fraction flag. Then tape your flag to a dowel. Wave your fraction flag proudly!

TIPS FOR A SUCCESSFUL PROJECT

◆ Encourage students to plan out their flags on scratch paper before they start drawing the lines.

◆ Here's a fun way to display the flags: Have students stand the flags up on their desks by sticking the flagpoles into small lumps of clay.

WANT TO KEEP GOING?

◆ Challenge students to try making a group of flags that show the same fraction in different ways. For example, all of the flags below show the fraction ¼:

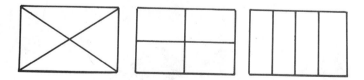

◆ Have your students look up international flags in an encyclopedia and make lists or draw pictures of the flags that are divided into fractional parts (e.g., Belgium = thirds; Burkina Faso = halves, etc.).

FRACTION QUILTS

Your whole class will "warm up" to fractions as you work together to make a beautiful quilt design.

WHAT YOU NEED

◆ one or more blank Quilt Squares for each student (reproducible page 86)

◆ two crayons or markers in different colors for each student (everyone must use the same two colors)—designate one color "Color One" and the other "Color Two"

WHAT TO DO

Student Instructions / *Teacher Notes*

1. **Take a look at your blank quilt square. It's divided into 32 equal triangles. Color in a fractional part of the triangles with Color One. Try to make a pattern as you color the triangles. Then color in the remaining triangles with Color Two.**

Choose a fraction of 32 for students to work with. If they are new at fractions, pick a simple one such as ½ or ¼. If you've worked with fractions before, use a tougher fraction such as ⅝ or 1 5/32. Before your students begin coloring, ask: How many triangles will you need to color with Color One? Once they have come up with the solution, encourage them to color in the triangles in a symmetrical fashion—that is, so that both sides of the quilt square look alike. Here are some ideas:

¼

½

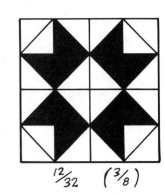

¹²⁄₃₂ (³⁄₈)

2. **When you and your classmates have created enough quilt squares to make a quilt, put all of the squares together.**

Have students color in the quilt squares until you have enough to make a square (you'll need 9, 16, 25, or 36) or a squarish rectangle (you'll need 12, 20, 30, or 42 quilt squares). Pin the squares in formation on a bulletin board and label it OUR ½ QUILT. Or tape the squares together and hang the quilt in the hallway for all to enjoy!

TIPS FOR A SUCCESSFUL PROJECT

◆ Encourage students to create as many different quilt square designs as they can using the same fraction.

◆ The quilts look best if every triangle is colored in—don't leave any white triangles.

WANT TO KEEP GOING?

◆ Now that students have seen what a fraction quilt looks like when each square is a different design, let them try making a fraction quilt in which all of the squares are the same. (This project will really emphasize the beauty and math behind quilting.) Here are some of the patterns your students might like to try:

½   ½   ¼

◆ Borrow a book on quilts from the library. Take a look at some of the patterns with students. Ask them to think about the number of squares that make up each quilt, and the fractional makeup of each individual square.

QUILT SQUARE

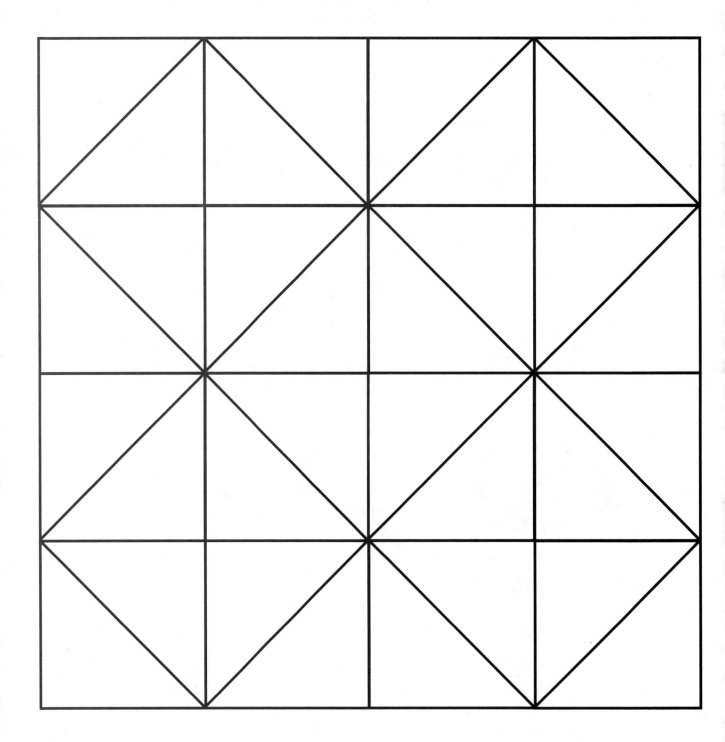

COLOR WITH FRACTIONS

Your students will watch clay change colors before their eyes when they find the missing fractional parts of a whole.

WHAT YOU NEED

◆ Color Recipe List for each student (reproducible page 89)

◆ red, yellow, blue, and white play clay

◆ measuring spoons in these sizes: ½ teaspoon, ¼ teaspoon, ⅛ teaspoon

WHAT TO DO

Student Instructions / *Teacher Notes*

1. Choose a color recipe from the list. Decide which fraction is missing from the problem.

If necessary, review halves, quarters, and eighths with students. Discuss the different ways that those fractions can combine to make a whole (a teaspoon, in this activity).

2. Once you have found the missing fraction, write it on the blank line. Then measure out the clay you will need with the correct size measuring spoons. Squish the different colors of clay together until it makes a solid color. Write the name of the new color in the space after the recipe.

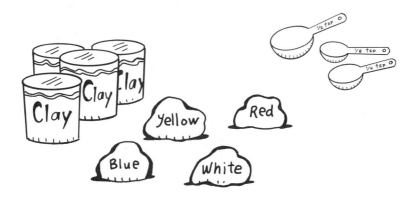

3. **Create each recipe on the list. Then make up your own recipes and colors!**

   Students will have more freedom creating their own colors if you don't require them to make the fractions add up to exactly one teaspoon. You may still require, however, that they add up the fractions in their recipes and express the total in terms of teaspoons.

4. **Use the different colors of clay to make crazy critters, clay rainbows, or colorful flowers. What else can you do with the clay?**

TIPS FOR A SUCCESSFUL PROJECT

◆ Ask students to bring in sets of measuring spoons from home. Depending on the number of measuring spoons you collect, students can work in groups and share them.

◆ Make sure students' hands (and the measuring spoons) are clean each time they begin mixing colors. That way, they won't add any dirt or extra colors to the clay. Also, remind them not to put the mixed colors back into the clay containers.

WANT TO KEEP GOING?

◆ Make a large chart listing all of students' recipes and the resulting colors.

◆ Try a similar activity using opaque paints instead of clay.

COLOR RECIPE LIST

1. $\frac{1}{2}$ teaspoon red +___teaspoon yellow = 1 teaspoon

Color: _____

2. $\frac{1}{2}$ teaspoon blue +___teaspoon yellow + $\frac{1}{4}$ teaspoon white = 1 teaspoon

Color: _____

3. ___teaspoon yellow + $\frac{1}{4}$ teaspoon red + $\frac{1}{4}$ teaspoon white = 1 teaspoon

Color: _____

4. $\frac{1}{2}$ teaspoon red + $\frac{1}{4}$ teaspoon blue +___teaspoon white + $\frac{1}{8}$ teaspoon white = 1 teaspoon

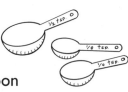

Color: _____

5. $\frac{1}{2}$ teaspoon blue +___teaspoon yellow + $\frac{1}{4}$ teaspoon yellow = 1 teaspoon

Color: _____

6. $\frac{1}{2}$ teaspoon red + $\frac{1}{4}$ teaspoon blue +___teaspoon yellow +___teaspoon white = 1 teaspoon

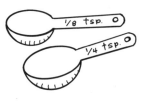

Color: _____

Make up your own fraction recipes here!

_____

_____

FRACTION SUNDAES

Here's a delicious way to help students visualize fractional parts of a group!

WHAT YOU NEED

◆ Fraction Sundaes Pattern for each student (reproducible page 93)

◆ construction paper in "ice cream" colors

◆ Ice Cream Flavor Color Combinations (reproducible page 91)

◆ tape

WHAT TO DO

Student Instructions / *Teacher Notes*

1. Cut out the sundae dish and set it aside.

2. Cut out the ice cream pattern. Trace the pattern as many times as you like on different colors of construction paper. Use the Ice Cream Flavor Color Combinations list for ideas. Each color will be a scoop of a different ice cream "flavor" for your sundae. Cut out the shapes.

Adjust the math level of this activity to students' skill level with fractions. Students who are new to fractions may need instructions as specific as "Put six scoops of ice cream on your sundae. One half of the scoops must be chocolate, and one half must be vanilla." Higher-level students can tackle problems such as "Put an odd number of scoops of ice cream on your sundae. Use five flavors of ice cream. Each flavor must represent a different fraction of the whole number of scoops."

3. Tape the scoops of ice cream to your sundae dish.

Tape the backs of the scoops of ice cream, overlapping them in front.

Back of sundae

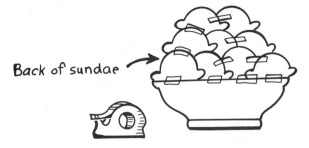

4. **Describe your sundae in fractions. How many scoops of ice cream does it have in all? That number will be the denominator of your fractions. How many scoops of each flavor does your sundae have? Those numbers will be the numerators of your fractions. List all the fractions on your sundae dish. Then top off your sundae with a red construction-paper cherry!**

Refer to the photo on page 90 to see how to label the sundae dishes.

TIPS FOR A SUCCESSFUL PROJECT

◆ Get students really excited about this project by inviting them to create their own wacky ice cream flavors and add the color combinations to their lists.

WANT TO KEEP GOING?

◆ Cut out lots of sundae dishes and scoops of ice cream. Hang up a list of "flavors" and set up an "ice cream parlor" in your classroom. Students can take turns serving one another. Or invite students from another class to visit your ice cream parlor and let them order sundaes by the fraction!

◆ Create a monster sundae on a bulletin board in your classroom. Have students contribute flavors until you have reached a certain number of scoops, such as 100. Then work together to figure out all of the fractions that make up the whole sundae. Check your work by adding up all of the numerators to make sure the total is the same number as the denominator.

Ice Cream Flavor
Color Combinations

strawberry = pink paper with red dots

chocolate chip = white paper with brown dots

cookie dough = white paper with tan dots

mint chocolate chip = green paper with brown dots

fudge ripple = white paper with brown stripes

bubble gum = pink paper with pink dots

pistachio = green paper with brown dots

FRACTION SUNDAES

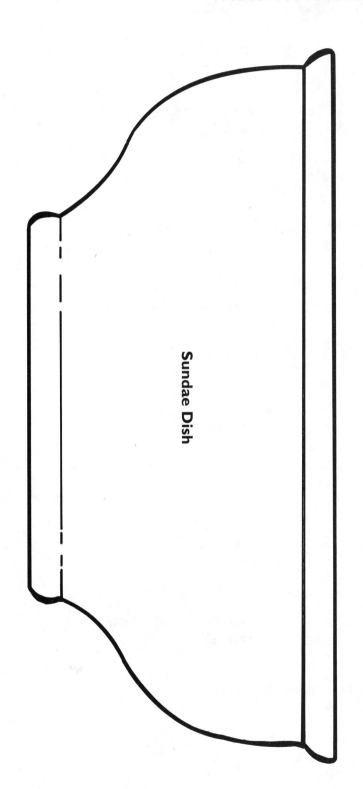

Sundae Dish

Ice Cream Scoop

Resources

Resources for Teachers

Easy Origami: Step-by-Step Projects that Teach Across the Curriculum
by Gay Merrill Gross and Tina Weintraub (Scholastic Professional
Books, 1995)

Fun with Pattern by Fifi Weinert (Metropolitan Museum of Art and
Viking Books, 1995)

The Hand Book of Creative Discovery and ***Making Things***
by Ann Wiseman (Little, Brown, 1973)

How to Make Super Pop-Ups by Joan Irvine (Beech Tree Books, 1992)

I Spy Two Eyes: Numbers in Art devised and selected by Lucy Micklethwait
(Greenwillow, 1993)

Kids Create! by Laurie M. Carlson (Williamson Publishing, 1990)

The Kids' Multicultural Art Book by Alexandra Terzian
(Williamson Publishing, 1993)

Make Gifts! by Kim Solga (North Light Books, 1991)

Math Power Magazine (Scholastic magazines; to order, call: (800) 631-1586)

Multicultural Books to Make and ***Share*** by Susan Kapuscinski Gaylord
(Scholastic Professional Books, 1994)

Multicultural Math: Hands-on Activities from Around the World
by Claudia Zaslavsky (Scholastic Professional Books, 1994)

My Nature Craft Book by Cheryl Owen (Little, Brown, 1993)

Patchwork Math 1: 100 Addition and Subtraction Reproducibles and
Patchwork Math 2: 100 Multiplication and Division Reproducibles
by Debra Baycura (Scholastic Professional Books, 1990)

Puddles and Wings and Grapevine Swings and ***Things to Make and Do
with Nature's Treasures*** by Imogene Forte and Marjorie Frank
(Incentive Publications, Inc., 1982)

Quilting Activities Across the Curriculum by Wendy Buchberg
(Scholastic Professional Books, 1997)

Literature for Students

Anno's Math Games and **Anno's Math Games II** by Mitsumasa Anno (Philomel, 1982, 1987)

Anno's Mysterious Multiplying Jar by Masaichiro and Mitsumasa Anno (Philomel, 1983)

The Canada Geese Quilt by Natalie Kinsey-Warnock (Cobblehill, 1989)

Eight Hands Round: A Patchwork Alphabet by Ann Whitford Paul (HarperCollins, 1991)

Grandfather Tang's Story by Ann Tompert (Crown, 1990)

Jumanji by Chris Van Allsburg (Houghton Mifflin, 1981)

The Keeping Quilt by Patricia Polacco (Simon & Schuster, 1988)

The Paper Crane by Molly Bang (Mulberry, 1985)

Paper John by David Small (Farrar, Straus & Giroux, 1987)

The Phantom Tollbooth by Norton Juster (Knopf, 1972)

Sweet Clara and the Freedom Quilt by Deborah Hopkinson (Knopf, 1992)

The Tangram Magician by Lisa Campbell Ernst (Abrams, 1990)

Tree of Cranes by Allan Say (Houghton Mifflin, 1991)

The Wheeling and Whirling-Around Book by Judy Hindley (Candlewick, 1994)

Arts-and-Crafts Supplies

You can order arts-and-crafts supplies such as beads, felt, pipe cleaners, decorative papers, glitter, sequins, and other materials from the companies listed below. Call for free catalogs.

S & S Crafts: (800) 243-9232

Oriental Trading Co.: (800) 228-2269

Notes